Original title:
A Brooch for the Brave

Copyright © 2025 Creative Arts Management OÜ
All rights reserved.

Author: Dexter Sullivan
ISBN HARDBACK: 978-1-80586-084-6
ISBN PAPERBACK: 978-1-80586-556-8

Medals of the Heart's Resolve

In a battle of love, she wore her shield,
Made of chocolate, it never squealed.
Fighting off foes with a grin so wide,
Her laughter, the weapon, her joy, the guide.

As foes approached in the dead of night,
She threw gummy bears, what a silly sight!
Medals of courage, they gleamed and sparkled,
While chocolates melted, their stories chuckled.

Enchantments of Resilience

With a wand made of noodles, she cast her spell,
Turning frowns upside down, oh can't you tell?
Her magic was messy, her potions were strange,
Yet every mishap brought laughter, not change.

In the midst of chaos, she danced on a chair,
Juggling pickles and jelly, without a care.
Enchantments of courage, in giggles they wrap,
While friends join her antics, what a delightful trap!

The Silver Star of Grit

With gum on her shoe, she trekked up the hill,
Barking like a dog, oh what a thrill!
Stars in her eyes as she slid in the grass,
The silver star glimmers, no moment to pass.

In the race to the top, she tripped on a rock,
But giggled aloud, for she couldn't be shocked.
The journey was quirky, the grit made her shine,
With every mishap, her spirit divine.

Beauty Forged in Fire

In a kitchen of chaos, she cooked with flare,
Her pasta caught fire; it flew through the air!
With a spatula mightier than swords from old,
She tamed her disasters, both funny and bold.

Beauty was forged in each wacky attempt,
Each dish that was burned, each moment that leapt.
In laughter she gathered, her spoons like a crown,
A queen in her kitchen, who never backs down!

The Fiery Crest of Valor

On a knight's chest, it shines so bright,
A silly spark in the heat of the fight.
With feathers and jewels, it sits with flair,
Who needs real armor when you've got a flare?

The dragon snorts, and the wizard laughs,
This shiny trinket? Oh, it has some gaffs.
'Wear it well, my friends!' the jester quips,
As he dodges the arrows and silly quips.

With every clash, it dances and twirls,
Around this knight, it leaps and unfurls.
The enemy stares, a confused gaze,
Wondering if style could end the craze.

At the end of the day, when the battles cease,
A sparkly trinket brought laughter and peace.
So here's to the crest, a showy delight,
In the world of the brave, it's a fashion fight!

An Adornment with Purpose

The captain wears it with pride and grace,
A trinket that says, 'I'm winning this race!'
With a wink and a nod, he takes to the field,
Sporting his badge, it's pure comedy revealed.

His soldiers chuckle, 'what's that you're wearing?'
He responds, 'It's magic, it's very endearing!'
With ribbons and sparkles that bounce in the light,
Who knew bravery could look so polite?

As arrows fly past, and the swords clash too,
His shiny medallion outshines every crew.
The foe in confusion can't take it no more,
Laughing so hard, they fall to the floor.

So here's to the one with the flamboyant flair,
In battles of courage, it's beauty we wear.
For in each brave heart, there's laughter to find,
An adornment with purpose, both bold and refined!

Grace Under Fire

In the pit of battle, all seems grim,
A brave knight trips, the odds grow slim.
He lands on his face, but laughs aloud,
With mud in his beard, he feels so proud.

His armor's shiny, yet pants are torn,
A fashion statement, though slightly worn.
With every tumble, he gains some flair,
For who's more daring than one with a dare?

Luminary of the Fearless

Behold the hero in mismatched socks,
With a cape made from grandma's old frocks.
Fearless and funny, he struts through town,
With laughter that turns the fiercest frown.

A valiant heart wrapped in a bright bow,
When trouble stirs, he steals the show.
His pet goldfish winks, just as bold,
This jester of valor will never be sold.

The Intrepid Emblem

In perilous quests, with jesters abound,
Our hero slips, yet grace is found.
A pie in the face, he takes it in stride,
With whipped cream laughter as his guide.

He battles dragons with silly retreats,
Trading his sword for some corny beats.
With banners that read, 'This is my style!',
His courage shines through, all the while.

A Flair for Fortitude

With a twirl of his cape and a wink of his eye,
He faces the foes, making them sigh.
A laugh and a jig when all seems lost,
The bravest of souls, but at what cost?

In a raucous dance that makes the ground shake,
He throws quite the punch, even if it's fake.
A hero of humor, the bravest of hearts,
With glittering sparkles and comical arts.

The Luminous Shield

In shiny metal, stories told,
Of daring deeds, brave and bold.
With every gleam, a laugh bestowed,
It guards the heart, yet makes you glow.

A knight adorned, with wink and jest,
In armor bright, he feels the best.
The sword may clash, but oh dear me,
His belt is tight! Now, that's the key!

Medallions of the Valiant

Twirling around, they spin and dance,
These glittering trinkets, pure romance!
Fear not the foe with gems so bright,
For laughter rings through every fight!

They jingle-jangle, oh what a sound!
As courage prances all around.
With every medal, a chuckle flies,
To conquer doubt, beneath blue skies!

A Symbol Beyond Fear

A shiny star upon the chest,
Brings forth the giggles, in the quest.
For who can frown while sporting flair?
Emboldened spirits, light as air!

With silly capes and armor bright,
The bravest hearts embrace the light.
Guffaws and grins, they dance with glee,
Bold adventures, come share with me!

The Emblematic Heart

A heart that shines, with laughter loud,
Standing firm, yet feeling proud.
It jests and jives, a playful spark,
While clearing paths through messy dark!

With every badge, a chuckle grows,
For sweets and treats are what he knows.
Through thick and thin, the humor flows,
A badge of fun, where courage glows!

Adornment of Courage

A shiny clip upon my shirt,
It holds the secrets of the flirt.
With every wink, it gives a cheer,
A dapper flair that quells all fear.

Upon my chest, it starts to sway,
A bold declaration of the day.
Of coffee spills and puppy paws,
It gleams through chaos, earns applause.

With colors bright, it's quite a sight,
It twinkles in the morning light.
A trusty buddy in the fray,
It dances with me all the way.

Token of the Bold

A funny shape, a wobbly form,
It's not quite normal, breaks the norm.
On days of dread, it saves my skin,
A trusty shield, let laughter in.

In meetings grim, it takes a stance,
With goofy glints, it leads the dance.
To every task that seems too tough,
It nudges me, 'Come on, that's enough!'

When faced with giants, fears might creep,
But this odd thing won't let me weep.
It sparkles bright, a silly tale,
In the bravest quests, I'll never fail.

Pinning Hopes

I found a pin beneath the drawer,
It's rusty, old, yet holds much more.
It tells of times when courage bloomed,\nAnd laughter chased away the gloom.

This funky gem, it shines so bright,
Awkward angles make it right.
Each twist and turn, a tale unfolds,
Of all the wonders gutsy souls hold.

With every pin that sticks around,
A merry tune is always found.
It dances on my workday woes,
A flag of courage where humor flows.

Ornament of the Undaunted

Upon my collar, there it sits,
A charming trinket with little knits.
A dash of flair on days of fright,
It whispers, "You'll be just alright."

In storms of doubt, it holds my hair,
And sends the wind a cheeky glare.
A bit of goof, a lot of grace,
It makes the world a better place.

Through mishaps grand and puddles deep,
It clings to hope, it makes me leap.
With every chuckle, there's a shove,
An ornament of dreams I love.

The Starlight Brooch

A brooch that twinkles bright,
It guides the lost at night.
With each bizarre little blink,
It winks, and makes you think.

In battlefields of fashion clout,
It shouts, 'Dare to stand out!'
With a sparkle and a jest,
It claims its fancy quest.

Worn by knights in armor bold,
With tales of bravery told.
But really, it just likes to shine,
And sip on sparkling wine.

So wear it on your chest with pride,
Let whimsy be your guide.
For in the laughter we fly,
With the starlight, oh so spry!

Bravery's Timeless Treasure

An emblem of the quirky kind,
It laughs, it giggles, never blind.
With every twist and glittering spin,
It's a treasure you just can't win.

It flaps in the wind like a cape,
Making the timid escape.
Each pointy bit tells a joke,
For those who dare provoke.

Oh brave soul with a wink so sly,
Clip this gem and fly high.
When courage starts to droop,
It's a riot; join the troop!

For bravery isn't always fierce,
Sometimes it's just to pierce,
The boring with a splash of glee,
And be as bold as we can be!

The Daring Pendant

A pendant round, so full of cheer,
It giggles softly in your ear.
With little tales of daring feats,
It dances to its tiny beats.

Worn by those with courage grand,
It plays tricks, makes life unplanned.
From meetings dull to coffee runs,
It's the life of all the funs!

Blushing brighter than a rose,
It teases with a silly pose.
"Oh look at me, so brave and bold,"
It says, "Just watch my stories unfold!"

So clip it on and strut your stuff,
In a world that's often tough.
For with laughter, we brave the day,
And stylishly, we find our way!

A Token of the Brave Journey

This token of courage, how it shines,
It tickles hearts and twists their spines.
Fastened on with a wink and grin,
It whispers, 'Let the fun begin!'

With every twist around your neck,
It gives the mundanity a check.
Each step you take with this delight,
Turns ordinary to outright flight!

From coffee spills to daring falls,
It catches laughter in the halls.
A brave companion that won't quit,
With punchlines dressed in a perfect fit.

So rally forth with style and glee,
This journey's best when brave and free.
For life is jest and gags that bloom,
With tokens bright that banish gloom!

Gems of Indomitable Spirit

In a world of grand delight,
Where courage wears a funny light,
A gem that laughs to shine so bright,
It twinkles in the dark of night.

With every challenge it will grin,
A cheeky wink as if to win,
It twirls around, a little spin,
Embracing all that lies within.

The bravest heart, it does endorse,
With a quirky, playful force,
It gives a nudge, ignites the course,
A friendship formed, a joyous source.

The Amulet of the Strong

An amulet with style unique,
It has some tricks, oh what a peak!
When heroes need it most, they seek,
A chuckle wrapped in bravery's cheek.

It bounces high, won't sit down straight,
Gives courage a delightful crate,
With every jest, it won't abate,
Embarking on a playful fate.

When battles rage and fears arise,
This charm will sport a bold disguise,
It throws confetti in the skies,
And fills the air with wild goodbyes.

The Enigma of Valor

An old enigma, twist and turn,
It guards the brave, but can't discern,
With every laugh, the flames will burn,
Daring souls for glory yearn.

In shadows deep it likes to hide,
Eager hearts, it won't abide,
With tickles, jokes, and laughter wide,
In valor's name, it's bona fide.

A riddle wrapped in courage's glow,
For those who dare and those who know,
It prances forth, a dashing show,
And to the brave, it steals the show.

The Glistening Mark of Courage

A glistening mark, oh such a jest,
It dances where the bravest rest,
With every grin, it feels the quest,
A badge of joy in life's fun fest.

When faced with foes, it makes a face,
A secret laugh, a wild chase,
Worn with pride, its warm embrace,
Will guide the brave in every place.

With every tale, it twirls and spins,
A sparkle bright that surely wins,
In laughter's grip, true courage begins,
A mark of fun where power grins.

The Jewel that Sparks Valor

In a land where courage's lost its way,
A trinket glimmers, brightening the fray.
It's not a sword, nor shield of famed delight,
But a shiny thing that makes the timid fight.

With a laugh it dances, glowing in the light,
Turning warriors' frowns into sheer delight.
They march with pride, as silly as can be,
Claiming valor's feathered hat, all for free!

What's in their pockets, treasures ain't the norm,
Just jangling keys, the humor's in the form.
Who knew the brave just need a little fun,
To face their fears and embrace the pun?

So wear this gem, let laughter light your way,
In every battle, silliness will sway.
For courage isn't always fierce and loud,
Sometimes it's sparks, hidden in the crowd!

A Talisman of Indomitable Hope

In the corner of the room, it starts to gleam,
A playful charm, more than it may seem.
With every chuckle, it spins tales anew,
Of heroes who danced while facing the blue.

This talisman whispers, 'Don't take it so tough,'
'Wear me, my friend, it's time to get rough!'
The bravest of hearts can laugh through the strife,
With absurdity mixed, they'll win this life.

As they stumble forward, dreams into reality,
The amulet giggles, spreading its vitality.
With a wink and a smile, they charm the night,
In every quirk, their spirits take flight.

So if the weight of the world feels too wide,
Just look for that spark, let your laughter guide.
Hope is a bubble, bursting in the air,
With a trinket in hand, all worries laid bare!

Unfurling Wings of Strength

Amidst the bleakness, a feather takes flight,
Not just for the bold, but for those who delight.
It's a wing of a chicken, not an eagle's grace,
But it carries the brave, all in one silly chase.

With each flap they stumble, oh what a parade!
Laughter erupts; no one's afraid.
They gather their courage, like pie on a plate,
Fluffy and funny, not quite first-rate.

These wings of whimsy teach strength with a twist,
To see the absurd, you can't dare to miss.
In moments of madness, the heart finds its song,
In the world of the brave, where laughter is strong.

So let's take to skies, with feathers of cheer,
And flap through the troubles that whisper near.
For in the dance of the quirky and free,
Strength is a jest that just needs to be!

The Radiance of Quiet Bravery

In a corner where shadows silently crawl,
There shines a light, one that tickles us all.
It glows with a grin, not hidden in fear,
With quiet bravado that brings us all cheer.

For bravery whispers, 'Let's giggle a tad,'
While facing the storms that might make us mad.
It's not the loud roar of lions at play,
But a chuckle that carries through every gray day.

Small deeds of valor wrapped in a joke,
A helping hand, or a warm-hearted poke.
In the calm of the night, or the whisper of dawn,
Radiance shines bright, let the laughter live on!

So hold on to this shimmer, silly yet bold,
In the dance of our hearts, let warmth unfold.
For it's the little things that make us stand tall,
Quiet bravery's glow, is the bright gem of all!

Grasping Glory

On a sunny day, he struts with flair,
His badge of honor pinned with care.
The wind, it gives a playful tug,
That shiny pin, a special mug!

In the office, he's a sight to see,
Crowds gather round, oh the glee!
But a coffee spill, oh what a fright,
His glorious brooch is now wet and bright!

Each step he takes, a jaunty dance,
His gleaming gem, a brave romance.
With every quirk, he steals the show,
Around his brooch, the wild tales grow!

Yet in the end, it's just a pin,
But who can resist that charming grin?
With laughter echoing, we all agree,
A hero's heart is the true marquee!

The Gritty Gem

In a dusty town where legends sprout,
A gem once lost, now found, no doubt.
　With grit and grime, it tells a tale,
　Of battles fought and foes so pale.

With a wink and nod, the hero prances,
Through muddy puddles, he takes his chances.
　The gem's rough edges sparkle bright,
　A little scruff brings pure delight!

He waves it high, oh what a sight,
The local kids cheer with sheer delight.
　With every laugh, he earns his fame,
　That gritty gem, a glorious claim!

Yet sometimes it falls and rolls away,
　Into obscurity, just for a day.
But with a chuckle and a gentle grin,
　He finds it back, let the fun begin!

Crest of the Intrepid

A crest so bold upon his chest,
With stories grand, it's truly blessed.
Through thorny paths and silly quirks,
The brave face laughter, that's how it works!

Adventurous hearts with wit so keen,
Defy the mundane, create the scene.
As they march on with toes a-tap,
Their crest ignites the playful clap!

When challenges loom like stormy skies,
They stand unwavering, oh how they rise!
With every jest and playful cheer,
The crest shines bright, no hint of fear!

So here's to hearts that boldly play,
With laughter ringing, come what may.
For every intrepid, quirky soul,
A crest awaits to make them whole!

Shimmering Shield

With a shimmering shield, he's ready to go,
Deflecting dullness, putting on a show.
In a world so gray, he adds the hue,
With every twinkle, he bids adieu!

Through the market, he struts with pride,
His shield reflects joy, no need to hide.
"Oh, what's that?" a vendor cries,
"Your shield's a gem!" amid all the sighs.

He winks and spins, doing a jig,
While the shield sparkles, it's all a big gig.
With laughter ringing and sweets in hand,
He conquers the day, oh isn't life grand?

A shield of fun, for battles unseen,
His shimmering charm, a lovely sheen.
For in this life of quirks and thrills,
The bravest hearts know laughter fulfills!

Radiant Resolve

On a chilly day, she brightened the gloom,
With a glittery pin that danced with a boom.
Her friends all laughed at her sparkly flair,
Claiming it helped her summon the air.

Squirrels would pause, with puzzled delight,
As she strutted along, a shimmering sight.
Bumblebees buzzed, enamored and bold,
Following her shine, a tale to be told.

Each twist and turn made her giggle in glee,
The brooch spun tales, wild as can be.
With every step, bravery swayed,
In a frolicsome dance, her worries delayed.

A knight in disguise, with a laugh, not a frown,
She wore her shimmer like a whimsied crown.
In a kingdom of laughter, where smiles entwine,
Her radiant resolve was simply divine.

The Courageous Keepsake

A thimble of courage, stitched in her side,
With buttons of bravery, there's nowhere to hide.
Her keepsake, a chuckle, a wink and a jig,
Like a pirate's treasure, oh what a gig!

The toaster agreed, with a pop and a cheer,
As toast flew high, filled with laughter and beer.
She wore it with pride, each day a parade,
Such daring attire, a glorious charade.

Friends gathered 'round and they just had to see,
A smorgasbord of trinkets, all wild and free.
Balloons in their hands, they bounced with delight,
As she twirled her keepsake, so bold in the light.

A daring grand romp, on a wobbly ride,
With her keepsake of courage, she danced inside.
With laughter on lips and hearts all ablaze,
Every moment with joy, she surely would praise.

Daring Sparkle

With a twinkle and spin, she caught all the eyes,
In a daring shimmer that heated the skies.
Friends gathered 'round, in curiosity rife,
As she jiggled her charm, bringing joy to life.

The pet cat was baffled, with wide-open stare,
At a dazzling display of her fanciful flair.
Her friends formed a line for a glimpse of the scene,
As prances and giggles became the routine.

Through puddles she splashed, with joy unconfined,
Her sparkle led hopscotch that danced in her mind.
With glittery winks, she conquered the day,
In a whirlwind of laughter, she found her own way.

Her daring sparkle, in moonlight so bright,
Turned ordinary moments into pure delight.
On this grand adventure, they all took a part,
Celebrating the brave, with a flick of her heart.

The Braveheart's Bauble

Once there was a bauble, so bold and so bright,
That danced on her dress in the shimmering light.
As she pranced through the town, with a wink and a grin,
The bauble told tales, infinite spin.

At lunch, it chimed in, with a bubbly tune,
While making the apples pretend they were moons.
A brave little heart beat within her delight,
As giggles erupted, taking flight like a kite.

It swayed in the breeze, like a band on parade,
Drawing all the smiles, in a grand escapade.
From dragons to unicorns, oh what a sight,
Her bauble created adventures all night!

With each jingle and twist, she spread magic untold,
In a kingdom of laughter, where the brave felt bold.
The bauble a beacon, igniting their spark,
In the heart of the brave, shining bright in the dark.

A Medal of the Unseen Battles

In shadows where the bravest hide,
They wear their smiles like armor bright.
With coffee cups and quickened stride,
They conquer mornings with delight.

Each glance a medal, gold or gray,
For victories where few can see.
In office wars, they save the day,
With staplers sharp, they set us free.

Behind the desk, they fight the grind,
With witty jokes and laughter loud.
In every task, true strength we find,
A secret army, brave and proud.

So raise a mug, cheer for the brave,
Who battle each mundane affair.
Their unseen fights, we gladly save,
For every laugh, a hidden flair.

Adornment of the Fearless Spirit

In quirky hats and mismatched socks,
Fearlessness finds its finest style.
With every quip that truly rocks,
They strut through life with cheeky smile.

From coffee spills to office pranks,
They wear courage like a badge.
In laughter's dance, they join the ranks,
Unfazed by fate's mischievous edge.

Their spirit shines, a dazzling spark,
In awkward selfies, captured zest.
Adorning joy, they leave a mark,
Showing us all how to jest.

So let us cheer for those who dare,
With every giggle and delight.
For life's small jokes, we boldly share,
Adorned in laughter, spirits light.

Crafts of Courageous Souls

With glue and scraps, they forge ahead,
Creating art from life's lost bits.
No fear of failure in their stead,
They navigate through crazy fits.

From paper planes to glitter bombs,
Their crafty hands know no refrain.
With giggles sweet, they weave their psalms,
Conquering all with playful gain.

In every project, laughter glows,
They spin the mundane into cheer.
Crafts that twinkle, shake, and pose,
Reflecting hearts that persevere.

So gather 'round our crafty friends,
Who turn the ordinary bright.
For in each whim, their laughter sends
A testament to joy and light.

A Token of Undaunted Dreams

In dreams where troubles twist and twine,
They stumble forth with goofy grace.
With every fumble, hearts align,
Who knew that fails could sweetly trace?

With pie in face and laughter shared,
Their courage blooms in playful jest.
Through every mishap, they've declared,
That fun, not fear, is truly best.

A token worn like joyful badge,
They frolic on, embracing fate.
With every slip, they start to hatch,
A legacy of love, innate.

So let us join in this grand scheme,
With silly songs and wobbly moves.
For every joyful, fearless dream,
Is painted bright with laughter's grooves.

Charms for the Unyielding

In armor made of laughter,
They strut through daily strife,
With shiny, silly trinkets,
That add some zest to life.

Each charm tells a story,
Of a mishap or a fall,
They twinkle like the stars at night,
Boldly laughing through it all.

They dance when winds get breezy,
And glitter in the sun,
For those who wear these badges,
Life's a jolly fun run.

So if you're feeling weary,
And dreams seem out of reach,
Just wear these quirky charms,
And let hilarity teach.

Adorned with Grit

With spikes and funky colors,
And doodads all around,
They sport a style so fearless,
Even chickens cheer profound.

Bling that fights off troubles,
With sass and lots of cheer,
These badges of ambition,
Count every little fear.

Adorned in iron laughter,
They sparkle with delight,
Conjuring up the courage,
To leap into the night.

So wear your grit with giggles,
Embrace the wild parade,
For those who strut with humor,
In life, they'll never fade.

The Sigil of Resilient Hearts

A badge shaped like a pancake,
With syrup on the side,
Worn by those adventurers,
Who embrace the silly ride.

Each loop tells of the giggles,
In battles with the socks,
And how they triumphed bravely,
While dodging all the knocks.

With hearts that beat in rhythms,
Of music and of joy,
They brandish this fine emblem,
Like a toast to every ploy.

So raise a toast to antics,
And wear your spirit bright,
For those with clever symbols,
Shine boldly, day and night.

The Pendant of Bold Adventures

A pendant shaped like pizza,
With toppings made of gold,
It swings and makes them giggle,
As stories are retold.

From bungee jumps to mishaps,
It glimmers through the air,
For every brave endeavor,
It's a slice of happy flair.

Each adventure has a sparkle,
A twinkle in the gloom,
With this bit of flashy jewelry,
You conquer every room.

So grab your quirky pendant,
And let the laughter soar,
For those who wear these treasures,
Life's a comic uproar.

The Sparkle of the Fearless

In a world where bravery shines,
A pin's placed on shirts, oh how it aligns.
With glimmering stones that dance and twirl,
Making heroes out of the shyest girl.

A clip on the collar, a charm on the hat,
It's all in good fun, imagine that!
When courage needs a little flair,
They sparkle and blink without a care.

With laughter and jokes, it eases the fright,
Each shiny adornment takes flight in the night.
For all who dare face their charming fears,
It's the trinkets that tickle and bring out the cheers.

So wear it with pride, let the laughter ring,
For bravery's folly is the best kind of bling.
Each sparkle a story, each shine a delight,
Let's toast to the bold who shine so bright!

Precious Artifacts of Resistance

In the drawer of duds, there hides a gem,
From grandmas and uncles, a little mayhem.
Resistant to doubt, just like the wearers,
These quirky brooches are laughable tearers.

One's shaped like a frog, another a star,
Each piece tells of battles, near and far.
Fashioned for warriors, with humor and grace,
They're tokens of triumph, each in its place.

A rainbow of colors, they wiggle and squirm,
While sitting on lapels, keeping spirits warm.
With every attachment, the tales unfold,
Of silly escapades and brave hearts bold.

Wear these artifacts, let giggles arise,
For laughter in conflict is a joyful surprise.
In the outfit of strength, they play their own role,
Precious equips for the fearless soul.

Keeper of the Braveheart

A tiny shield rests on the chest,
It guards against fears with charming jest.
With glittering eyes, it winks at the foe,
Reminding brave hearts to put on a show.

This tiny protector, with flair it abounds,
Holds courage like jellybeans, oh so profound!
A squishy affection wrapped up in a clasp,
It makes you feel buoyant, like air in a gasp.

There's wisdom in laughter, a soft gentle poke,
This emblem of bravery makes life less choke.
So let it be known that in silly attire,
A keeper of courage can spark a wild fire!

For when humor reigns, and worries digress,
The keeper of hearts wears laughter, no less.
And in every twinkle, a story takes flight,
Brave hearts united, glowing delight!

The Glimmer of Resolve

A little shiny thing, it shines so bright,
Caught in the spotlight with all of its might.
With quips and glances, it sets the tone,
Wrestling with worries as light as a bone.

On jackets and purses, it plays peek-a-boo,
A spark of conviction shining right through.
Every glimmer a giggle, every shine a cheer,
A laugh in resistance, becoming quite clear.

Amid the concerns and the challenges faced,
This little badge of honor is perfectly placed.
With humor as armor, the brave strut about,
Emblazoned in laughter, they dance and they shout.

So here's to that sparkle, to mischief and fun,
To every brave heart that bubbles and runs.
In the laughter they conquer, the fun never fails,
With glimmers of resolve, they ride on the trails!

Mementos of the Valiant Soul

In the drawer lies a badge too bright,
Worn by the brave on a Friday night.
It sparkles and shines, oh what a sight,
But it pokes at my shirt, oh what a fright!

With each step it jangles, a metallic tune,
I strutted so proud, I felt like a loon.
The knights of old would surely attune,
To a hero's plaque that got up and swooned!

When a ghost dared to loiter near my shoe,
I waved it around, claimin' my due.
But it flicked me instead, oh what a view,
Guess I shouldn't have challenged that boo!

So if you find valor in objects you keep,
Just remember, they might cause you to weep.
Bravado's all fun, but who knew the leap,
Would land you in trouble, a tumble, a heap!

The Pin that Shimmers with Bravery

This little pin has seen better days,
It's tarnished and bent in so many ways.
It's a relic of courage, or so it conveys,
Yet it leads me to mischief in hilarious plays.

When I wore it to work, the boss had to smirk,
Called me a legend, but missed the real perk.
At lunch it flew off, oh what a big jerk:
Now it rests on my sandwich, how's that for a quirk?

Tales of the past, like dragons and quests,
This pin holds a story that surely invests.
But back to the kitchen, where mystery rests,
It's lost in the soup, and I must confess!

Now I claim it's a weapon of culinary flare,
"Defender of dips!"—I proudly declare.
A kitchen crusader, beyond all compare,
Yet I burn the toast, so no one will care!

Tokens of the Dauntless Dreamer

A tiny token, bright like a star,
Sometimes it's fancy, most times bizarre.
I wear it with pride, but it's left quite a scar,
When I accidentally called it a fruit jar.

With every adventure, it tags right along,
In battles of boredom, it helps me feel strong.
But it fell in the toilet—what could go wrong?
Now it's just smelly, and I sing a sad song.

Its charm's unforgettable, if slightly a mess,
My buddies all chuckle, oh what a distress.
For a warrior's gelt, it brings not success,
Unless you count laughter as part of the quest!

So here's to the tokens we boldly bring forth,
To cheer up the days, for better or worse.
For laughter's the treasure, that's what it's worth,
Even if it's stuck in your pocket—oh curse!

Radiance in the Face of Fear

When dawn breaks with giggles, courage takes flight,
My shining accessory gives foes a fright.
It sparkles so bright, like a disco at night,
Yet it sweats on my shirt, now that's not polite!

Worn on my collar, it looks like pure gold,
But it tries to escape when the stories are told.
It leaps from its perch—oh how bold!
Now it's stuck in a sandwich; my fate's uncontrolled!

The bravest tales always come with a twist,
But mine's just a misfit, you get the gist.
We treasure the sparkles; we shake our fists,
When bravery means wearing a pin on your wrist.

So raise up your voices and laugh without fear,
For pins can be funky; that much is clear.
Strength isn't just serious—it can be sincere,
And sometimes it's laughter that brings us good cheer!

An Adornment for the Fearless Journey

Upon my chest, it sparkles bright,
A flimsy charm that takes to flight.
It claims to keep the fears at bay,
    But trips me up in silly play.

With every step, it jangles loud,
A brave fashion that draws a crowd.
They laugh and cheer, it's quite the sight,
    A daring heart in clumsy flight.

The fabric flaps like wings of birds,
As I recite courage in words.
Falling flat but dressed to amaze,
    A fearless show in funny ways.

So strut my stuff, a sight to see,
In dazzling flair, I'm wild and free.
With each mishap, a joyous cheer,
    An adornment bold, I persevere.

The Shimmer of Defiant Dreams

A twinkling gem in dreams displayed,
With hopes and laughs, my fears betrayed.
Its shiny glow, a wink of fate,
I wear it proudly, though it's late.

In every step, my style's a joke,
It may just be a silly cloak.
But laughter is a charming shield,
And that's the armor my dreams wield.

It wobbles like a jelly fish,
A wondrous tale of what I wish.
Defy the night with gleaming grace,
With sparkles bright in every space.

So here I stand, a glimmering sight,
In dreams that dazzle, bold and bright.
Defiant hearts may laugh and scheme,
With shiny gems that stir the dream.

Relics of Courageous Deeds

I found a relic, oh what a thing,
A tattered charm with a rubber ring.
It tells of fights, of running race,
In a wobbly plastic, it finds its place.

Each dent and ding holds tales unknown,
Of daring acts and seeds they've sown.
With whimsy's grace, it sits atop,
Bold and bizarre, I'll never stop.

I strut about, a walking tale,
With every laugh, I cannot fail.
A champion's heart in splendid mode,
With relics bright upon the road.

So grab your charms and join the fleet,
In funny tales, we cannot be beat.
With relics grand, we make our mark,
In courage's name, we light the spark.

The Token of Fearless Acts

Here's a token for the brave and bold,
A trinket loud with stories told.
It jiggles as I dance around,
With every laugh, new joy is found.

I wear it proudly on my sleeve,
A funny badge, I truly believe.
That courage blooms in quirky ways,
With silly acts, it surely stays.

Each wobbly step, a laugh is had,
With token bright, I'll never be sad.
For fearless acts may cause a grin,
Like stumbling clowns, we all begin.

So grab your tokens, join my spree,
In jovial jaunts, we wander free.
Celebrate with gin and snacks,
With tokens true of fearless acts.

Adornments of the Unyielding Spirit

A badge of honor, shiny and bright,
Just like my courage, ready to fight.
With every laugh, it winks with glee,
Marking my wins, just wait and see.

A lopsided pin, oh what a find,
Clashing colors, but it's one of a kind!
Each quirk adds charm, like my bold heart,
Together we're quirky, never apart.

Oh, what a joy, this gem I wear,
Flaunting my zeal, without a care.
It jingles and jives as I prance about,
"Look at me!" it shouts, filled with clout.

So here's to all, both silly and grand,
Those daring souls with style so planned.
With every sparkle, let laughter ring,
For unyielding spirits, we'll always sing!

Trinkets of Valor

A charm with a story, oh what a sight,
It danced on my jacket, in the moonlight.
A quirky blue owl, with googly eyes,
Perched on my shoulder, ready to surprise.

An acorn-shaped pendant, brave and bold,
Claiming my heart and never feeling old.
Its nutty wisdom, amusing and true,
"Grow past your worries; just look to the view!"

With jangles and giggles, my trinkets display,
A blend of whimsy saving the day.
For every time life gives me a poke,
These laughable gems make laughter provoke.

So gather your treasures, don't leave them behind,
For the bold and the brave, are perfectly aligned.
Each spark can remind us of moments so bright,
With humor and panache, let's dance through the night!

The Jewel of Daring

A sparkling bauble, sat upon my chest,
Looks like a fortune cookie on a quest!
Glimmers of fortune, wrapped in a grin,
Tickling my heart—let the fun begin!

It's adorned with a charm of glitzy flair,
Reminds me to venture, not just to stare.
With every twinkle, it shakes loose my frown,
"Be bold, be merry!" it sings, loud as a clown.

Oh, the mishaps, the fumbles, we cherish so dear,
With this dandy jewel, I'll conquer my fear.
Like lollipops rolling, I'll skip and I'll sway,
Courage is sweet, come join in the play!

So here's to our treasures, both silly and wild,
To every brave soul, every daring child.
With laughter as armor, let's shine on our way,
Embrace the absurd and make every day!

Ornaments of the Bold

A goofy giraffe, perched tall on my hat,
It wobbles and nods, just look at that!
Holding stories of courage behind every turn,
A whimsical symbol, that helps me learn.

Glittering buttons from adventures past,
Represent tales where we've had a blast.
Each stitch is a joke sewn into my soul,
Together we thrive, we make a whole.

On days of gray clouds, my trinkets resound,
With laughter and light, hopes spinning around.
From wacky to wise, they shout "Be bold!",
In every shiny piece, a story unfolds.

So flaunt your odd treasures, wear them with pride,
For the brave and the fun, we're all on a ride.
Let's gather our quirk, our laughs, and our cheer,
With each funny trinket, we'll banish the fear!

Emblem of Valor

A shiny pin upon my chest,
Displays my courage, I must confess.
It wobbles and shakes, oh what a sight,
I wear it proudly, feeling so bright.

In battle's midst, I lose my hat,
But this brave emblem? Now that's where it's at!
It jangles and jingles with every stride,
While I trip on my shoelaces—what a wild ride!

It's just a trinket, but here's the jest,
I strut like a king while feeling like a pest.
Though I'm not a knight, I act the part,
With this silly pin, I've captured my heart.

So here's to my brooch, my knightly swag,
It may be just metal, but it makes me brag.
Onlookers laugh, and I can't complain,
For bravery's charm comes wrapped up in gain!

The Heart's Armor

A heart-shaped token, stuck on my sleeve,
Sometimes a blessing, often a tease.
It glimmers in sunlight, makes me feel bold,
Yet sticks to my shirt like it thinks it's gold.

With every adventure, it shimmers and shakes,
It's a silly distraction, but that's what it makes.
Dodging the raindrops, I gallop in glee,
While my heart's armor yells, 'Look at me!'

Sometimes it flops, and sometimes it flips,
With my shirt's button, it performs acrobatic grips.
"Oh look, a hero!" my neighbor does say,
As I stumble and grin, "Just saving the day!"

So here's to my heart, a true funny shield,
With laughs and mishaps, its power I wield.
Though it's just a pin, it fuels my charm,
I'll wear it forever, and that's no alarm!

Trinket of the Fearless

A tiny trinket, bright red and bold,
It claims to keep fear—if only that's told.
I wear it with pride, though it constantly flops,
Like a long lost sock, or some weird candy drops.

With every step, there's a rattling sound,
As if bravery's marching right round and around.
People all chuckle, they can't help but smile,
As I strut like a general, if only a while.

It doesn't protect from my kitchen mishaps,
Or the grocery cart that always seems to collapse.
But it shines bright on my chaotic dress,
"Look at that gallant one!" Oh, what a mess!

So here's to my trinket, so brave and so free,
With laughter and giggles, it's perfect for me.
In the realm of clumsiness, I take my stand,
With this silly object, my heart is so grand!

Jewel of the Gallant

A jewel of courage, perched on my tie,
It winks like it knows all the reasons why.
While I tell my tales of brave nights and fights,
It reminds me of pizza on those relaxed nights.

"Where's your armor?" they ask with a grin,
"Oh, I left it home, but I've got this gem in!"
It's small and it sparkles, but oh what a clout,
As I trip over nothing, the crowd will shout!

With each silly story, I beam with delight,
As my jewel keeps laughing in the warm moonlight.
"Onward, brave soldier!" I call with a laugh,
While my jewel just rolls, saying "Who needs a gaffe?"

So here's to the sparkle that keeps me afloat,
It's a silly small gem, but it helps me gloat.
In a world full of fear, I stand with great pride,
With my funny little jewel, I'll never hide!

Embers of the Untamed

In a forest wild and free,
A squirrel wore my car key.
It glimmered bright, a sight to see,
I thought it was a treasure from tree to tree.

With acorns fierce, he roamed with pride,
A little bandit full of guide.
He showed off flair that cannot hide,
While we laughed, our worries set aside.

His bravery sparked, like autumn's flame,
In nutty battles, he'd stake his claim.
He took the prize, but what a game,
The furry champ, a legend's name!

Among the leaves, he did parade,
In goofy glory, unafraid.
The bravest rogue, with mischief laid,
A tale of valor, fun conveyed.

The Badge of Fortitude

A lion roared, with quite a flair,
He wore a badge, beyond compare.
But 'twas a paper plate, oh dear!
'The King of Puns!' we gave a cheer.

He strutted proud in the savannah sun,
With glittering glue, he'd had his fun.
'What do we hunt?' he'd spring and run,
'Let's find the snacks! Oh, yeah, my pun!'

In clever games, he'd claim his space,
Like sassy jokes, his wild embrace.
Each time we laughed, he won the race,
A comedic heart, with courage in grace.

When others took him with a frown,
His paper plate would never down.
For in our hearts, he wore the crown,
The bravest lion of this town!

Grace Worn by the Bold

A penguin strutted with a flair,
In tuxedo suit, he didn't care.
With mischief playing in his stare,
He slipped and slid, a dance so rare.

He belly-flopped with such delight,
In icy pools, he'd hop and bite.
Navigating fish with all his might,
What a spectacle, a wondrous sight!

With waddle grace, he took his stand,
In frosty winds, a brave command.
He gathered friends, a wacky band,
And led them off to frolic land.

Though chilly days would come and go,
The fun ignited, always in tow.
His heart a blaze, a goofy glow,
With every slide, their laughter would grow.

Radiant Armor of the Heart

A snail adorned with shiny shells,
Claimed he wore knightly battle bells.
With bold bravado, he rang and knells,
"Behold my might!" he sang with yells.

He paraded slow on one fine day,
On a leaf so grand, he led the way.
His friends quipped, "Look, isn't he gay?
A warrior slow, but never gray!"

In tiny jousts, they took their place,
As laughter echoed, setting the pace.
With tiny feats, they ran the race,
Their hero, slow, yet full of grace.

So lift your glass and hear their tale,
Of armored hearts that will not fail.
For bravery comes in many scales,
With little snails who'll always prevail!

Symbol of the Unyielding

In a world where heroes clash,
They wear a pin and never rash.
A sparkly shine on their attire,
Made from spoons and a bit of wire.

Laughing loud in YouTube fame,
A wannabe in a superhero game.
With capes flapping and pants too tight,
They march along, oh what a sight!

Like that cat who brave would leap,
But land, oh dear, right in a heap.
A badge of courage made to jest,
With wobbly knees, they face the test.

So here's to those who wear the flair,
With mismatched socks and wild hair.
Their brooches shine from all they boast,
In laughter, they become the host.

Courage's Crown

A crown of tin atop their head,
They prance about, no hints of dread.
With laughing eyes, they greet the day,
Chasing clouds in a quirky way.

"Onward, brave" the echoes call,
While tripping over their best friends' shawl.
Who knew that courage came in styles,
With silly hats and goofy smiles?

Through tightrope walks on garden hoses,
They leap for joy, ignoring poses.
For what's a hero without some flair?
They dance along without a care.

The throne of laughs, it is their gain,
Reigning over joy, they'll never wane.
With every laugh and every sound,
In silliness, their hopes are found.

Resilience in Radiance

With sparkles bright, they step outside,
In mismatched shoes, they dare to glide.
A twinkle here, a giggle there,
In every mishap, they're a flare.

In muddy boots, they brave the storm,
Their style's a mix, yet feels so warm.
With wobbly hearts and playful cheers,
They forge ahead, ignoring fears.

"Oh dear!" they shout, "What a grand fall!"
Yet chuckles flow in the loudest call.
For every slip, there's joy to find,
In trails of laughter, love is blind.

The radiant glow of silly grace,
A mirror ball in a glum place.
In each wrong turn, they make it bright,
With every laugh, they take to flight.

Badge of the Fearless

A pin upon their fluffy coat,
Declares they're brave, or maybe wrote.
With every bounce, a tale appears,
Of silly dreams and chuckled fears.

In epic fails, they take a stand,
With ice cream cones still in their hand.
Who needs a sword or flashy gear?
A sprinkle here, a grin, and cheer!

Through whispered doubts, they dance and prance,
With two left feet, they steal the chance.
In every giggle, you'll find the clue,
Courage is simple, and funny too.

So here's to those with laughter loud,
Who form a brave and silly crowd.
With badges bright and hearts aglow,
They'll make you laugh, as they steal the show.

The Insignia of the Fearless

In the heart of the night, a badge shines bright,
A twist of fate, and oh what a sight!
It wobbles and jiggles, makes laughter abound,
A testament of courage, in giggles it's found.

With every adventure, it dances with flair,
Stuck on a shirt, or caught in your hair.
It bravely proclaims, 'I've faced my own fears!'
But whispers it softly, over popcorn and beers.

The steadfast symbol, of odd escapades,
Of tripping on stairs and bizarre charades.
In sketches of glory and tales that won't quit,
This quirky old emblem, we humorously admit.

Now treasure this token, keep it in view,
For those daring moments, when laughed as you blew.
A token of bravery, though silly it may be,
This emblem of joy, you'll wear joyfully free.

Starlit Symbols of Strength

Twinkling like stars, on a cloak of the bold,
Each patch tells a story, both silly and told.
One's shaped like a donut, the other a cat,
A nod to our foibles, imagine that!

The night is alive with laughter and flair,
As warriors assemble, no worries or care.
They chase down the heroes, those socks on their hands,
Confetti of courage, in whimsical bands.

With stamps of bravery, let's celebrate fun,
Each twirl and each dance, we're never outdone.
In tales spun with giggles, no fear holds its place,
We'll wear these patches with humor and grace.

So gather your pals, let's create our own show,
Let's craft silly symbols, let the good times flow!
In a world of wild dreams, let's never forget,
The laughter we share is the bravest of bets.

Accolades for the Audacious

With ribbons of laughter, we hand out our praise,
To those who dare venture through peculiar ways.
One wedged in a cactus, one gets lost in grass,
Their tales of bold antics will forever outlast.

Each nod and each chuckle, a badge in our mind,
For mischief and mayhem, with friendships aligned.
Spilling out snacks while they're scaling a chair,
Brave warriors of humor, with flour on their hair.

They climb every mountain of ice cream so sweet,
With cones in their hands, they're never discreet.
In glittering moments, where silliness reigns,
Their laughter is armor, far greater than chains.

Raise toast to the silly, the brave and the bright,
For they're the true legends, who comfort the night.
With accolades given, to each bumpy ride,
These champions of light, they'll never subside.

The Luminary's Keeper

A star on the badge, where humor takes flight,
The keeper of laughter, it glimmers with light.
With capes made of pillows, their antics unfold,
In battles of tickles, a sight to behold.

Adventures of blunders, they dance and they play,
With pockets of giggles, they light up the way.
Through pudding and chaos, they boldly will roam,
The luminary keeper, dragging us home.

A flicker of courage, in quirky designs,
In capes made from sheets and mismatched shoelaces.
They'll leap o'er the puddles and skip past the frowns,
The power of joy in their comical crowns.

So let's toast to the goofy, the brave and the wacky,
For the best of our heroes, they make life feel snappy.
In laughter we gather, our spirits take flight,
With pins on our jackets, we glow through the night.

The Radiant Jewel of Tenacity

In the closet, it sits, so bold,
A shiny relic, with tales to be told.
It sparkles with grit, a brave little gem,
Dodging all doom, just like a diadem.

On a daring dress, it takes its stand,
An emblem of laughs, a quirky band.
Through coffee spills and wild dance breaks,
It holds its shine, despite all the shakes.

With humor in hand, it winks with flair,
Telling tales of adventures without a care.
A tiny warrior on cotton so bright,
It rallies the bold, igniting the night.

So wear it with pride, let your laughter blend,
With the tales of courage that never end!
Its heart beats with joy, tales never quite tame,
The jewel of tenacity, forever its claim.

Adorning the Brave

A tiny shield rests right on your chest,
Promising laughter when you need it best.
With every catch of the light, it glows,
Spurring on brave souls, as everyone knows.

It sparkles like mischief, it twinkles with fun,
Each hero adorned, feeling like number one.
From battles with socks to shoes on the run,
It jazzes up life until the day's done.

In meetings, it chuckles, lightly awry,
As the brave ones confess they might just fly high.
"Who needs a cape when you've got this charm?"
It giggles in silence, it means you no harm.

So wear your own armor, quirky and spry,
For adorning the brave, it's never too shy.
Brightening bits of the mundane parade,
This jeweled companion, how mischief is made!

The Ornament of Defiance

With sass and a wink, it jumps right to play,
A glimmering rebel, brightening the gray.
It takes on the world, with humor's embrace,
Turning dull moments into a fun race.

From blunders at brunch to epic fails wide,
This ornament laughs, it won't run or hide.
Sporting a grin, on a shirt it parades,
This badge of defiance, and fun never fades.

When nerves start to tingle, and hijinks ensue,
This cheerful sparkler whispers, "You'll get through!"
For the brave, unfazed by learning the ropes,
They wear their defiance, twinkling with hopes.

So let the world chuckle, let giggles ignite,
With the ornament of defiance, we'll dance through the night.
In a sea full of serious, it's splashed with a jolt,
Giggling through chaos, and never one fault!

The Fierce Brooch of Hope

A fearless pin, it fastens on tight,
A badge of the bold, ready for flight.
It laughs in the face of each looming task,
With a wink and a grin, it's no need to ask.

In meetings, it shimmers, a secret delight,
As it keeps up the spirit, making all bright.
Fierce as a lion, with hope in its heart,
This quirky creation is the best kind of art.

From lunch to the dance floor, it glimmers a cheer,
Reminding all wearers to shed every fear.
"Let's mix up the mundane!" it practically shouts,
With hope, laughter, and joy it proudly spouts.

So attach it with pride, let your colors burst,
With the fierce brooch of hope, quench the serious thirst.
In the laughter and fun, it finds its true role,
Wearing smiles of courage brightens the soul!

The Stalwart Gem

In feathered hats and shiny shoes,
They march with flair, they dance, they cruise.
A tiny gem upon their chest,
With winks and grins, they jest the best.

With every poke and silly cheer,
They face their foes, despite their fear.
That little sparkle, loud and brave,
A beacon for the quirkiest knave.

Through pies thrown fast, and pranks to spare,
They fight with laughter, full of flair.
That tiny jewel, oh what a sight,
A badge of honor, wrapped in light.

They strut and prance, so full of glee,
With every step, they claim victory.
Their hearts are bold, their spirits high,
With giggles echoing through the sky.

Spark of Valor

A glimmer shines, in colors bright,
A playful laugh, a friendly fight.
With every mischief, every tease,
This spark ignites, puts minds at ease.

Shaped like a pineapple, wild and round,
Worn by the brave, who dance unbound.
With jests and jibes, they take the lead,
In their own way, they plant the seed.

Each knock and tumble, each twist and turn,
From every stumble, new smiles they earn.
A beacon of fun, a vibrant token,
With every laugh, no spirit broken.

So raise a toast to their high cheer,
To the jokers who have no fear.
For in their hearts, with no disguise,
Lies a spark that lights the skies.

Memento of the Valiant

A badge of quirks, a wink of fate,
Worn by the brave, oh how they skate!
Through laughter bursting, joy supreme,
A memento wrapped in a wild dream.

With cupcakes flying, and pies on heads,
They spread their fun, like swarming threads.
Though foes may glare, they stand and grin,
For every battle, they just dive in.

Their spirits rise above the fray,
With every pun, they seize the day.
A tiny token of bravery shown,
In silly antics, their courage's grown.

So here's to those, the jesters of pride,
In sparkling garb, they stand side by side.
With laughter loud, and hearts that soar,
Their memento shines forevermore.

The Bold Talisman

A twinkling charm on every coat,
That silly badge, a real funny moat.
With pranks galore, they take the helm,
Our boldest knights in a silly realm.

A rubber chicken, perched just right,
Worn by the brave, who dance with might.
A spark of joy, a flicker bright,
In every jest, they claim their light.

With laughter ringing, they lead the way,
In chaotic storms, they laugh and play.
Those gallant hearts, so full of glee,
With every chuckle, they roam free.

So let them flaunt their wacky pride,
With every twist, they'll never hide.
In this grand tale, both bold and grand,
The talisman shines, oh isn't it grand!

The Defiant Dazzle

Amidst the flicker, a spark does shine,
A trinket that mocks, oh so divine.
With shimmering wit and a wink of flair,
It dares all faces, for laughter to share.

A shiny little jest, perched on a coat,
Winks at the doubtful, makes courage float.
For in its glow, the meek then jest,
Transforming the timid into the blessed.

It twinkles and giggles at solemn frowns,
Turning the mundane into playful crowns.
A pop of color in the dreary,
With every chuckle, making hearts cheery.

So wear it with pride, let your spirit prance,
For humor and bravado love to dance.
A little accessory, bold and bright,
Making every moment feel just right.

The Gleam of Brave Intentions

Brightly it shimmers, a daring charm,
Inspiring laughter, the sweetest balm.
With every glance, it spins a tale,
Of heroes and jesters who absolutely prevail.

No need for swords or a grand parade,
Just this little gem, a masquerade.
In pockets and purses, it finds its place,
Winking with optimism, a smile on its face.

When doughty hearts fear, it takes the stage,
In its playful shimmer, they turn the page.
Laughter erupts where bravery blooms,
As courage in laughter vanquishes glooms.

So hold it close, let it guide your quest,
For humor in valor is truly the best.
With gleeful intentions, take on the day,
Clad in the shine of a daring play.

Courage's Silent Witness

Nestled upon lapels, quiet yet bold,
A tale of valor, silently told.
A twinkle of mischief that speaks of grace,
In a world where laughter finds its place.

It keeps its secret, this tiny delight,
Watching bravado chase the night.
Through chuckles and sighs, it stands tall,
A silent cheerleader for all, for all.

When troubles arise, it winks from above,
Whispering bravery wrapped in love.
Let the world fumble, let worries unlace,
For here dwells a spirit that sets the pace.

So lighten your heart, let your worries cease,
With a charm that knows humor can bring peace.
With every spark, it declares its stance,
In the theater of life, all deserve a chance.

A Gleam that Inspires

Sparkling and lively, it catches the eye,
Drew a smile here or a giggle nearby.
In moments of doubt, it dances with glee,
A beacon of fun, wild and free!

Oh, how it glistens on a rainy old day,
Turning the mundane into a fun ballet.
With cheeky radiance, it lights the room,
Dancing laughter that swallows the gloom.

Inscribed in its shine is a spirit that dares,
To turn every struggle into whimsical flares.
For courage is playful, a jest at its heart,
And joy, oh dear friend, is a true work of art!

So clasp it with pride, give life a good shake,
For the bravest of hearts often simply partake.
In silly bravado and giggling delight,
With each gleam it offers, who needs to fight?

Courageous Charms of the Heart

In pockets deep, where treasures hide,
A button brave, with leaps of pride.
It tells the tales of daring falls,
With laughter echoing through the halls.

On shirts it shines, a tiny knight,
It chuckles back at fearsome fright.
When storms might brew and shadows loom,
It winks and teases, clears the gloom.

With quirks and jests, it'll cheer the day,
A tiny comrade, come what may.
No dragons here, just jolly jest,
Adventures wait, the heart's request.

So pin it on, and wear it bold,
A charm of fun, worth more than gold.
In every laugh, in every cheer,
This little gem, a hero's gear.

A Pendant for the Unbreakable

Hanging low, a jolly grin,
It glimmers bright through thick and thin.
With every swing, a punchline made,
A pendant full of laughter's trade.

When troubles rise, it shakes its head,
And tickles all the thoughts instead.
Who needs a cape when you can dangle
A bead of joy that makes you jangle?

With every twist, a daring jest,
It whispers secrets, doing its best.
Unbreakable? Well, that's the point,
A charm that brings the brave to joint.

So swing it wide, let laughter ring,
In trials tough, it's the fun thing.
For every soul that feels a fright,
This merry piece will be the light.

The Crest of Unflinching Will

Upon the chest, a badge of cheer,
Where courage greets the meek and sheer.
A crest that laughs at every frown,
It proudly sports a silly crown.

In battles won or lost, who cares?
It shines with mischief, paints with flares.
When courage falters, it gives a quip,
With every tilting, a joyous trip.

With fabric soft and humor bright,
It holds the dreams that take to flight.
The bravest hearts don't need to fight,
Just wear a grin and share the light.

So lift your chin, wear on your sleeve,
The crest of laughs, you better believe.
For in the chuckle, strength is found,
A funny charm, forever bound.

Trinkets of Triumph

Little trinkets, small and bright,
They sparkle gaily in the light.
Each one tells a tale so grand,
Of silly quests across the land.

From paperclips to buttons round,
Each holds a story, skillfully found.
In every shine, there's courage true,
A laugh to share for me and you.

Not gold nor silver, but giggles strong,
These playful pieces are where you belong.
For when you feel the world is tough,
A trinket's charm is just enough.

So gather these in joyful bunch,
And wear them with a merry hunch.
For with each laugh, a triumph sings,
In fun and joy, the heart takes wings.

The Jewel of Tenacity

In a world of daring feats,
A shiny pin takes center seat.
It's stuck on shirts, so proud and bright,
But endures the wrong washing night!

With each brave deed, it twinkles wide,
Yet gets snagged when I run and hide.
I wonder if it's got a plan,
To catch the threads of every man?

A knight in armor, made of flair,
Though sometimes lost behind a chair.
It's got my back in all the fray,
And brings a smile to every day!

Though it's just a glimmer in my stash,
It's worth a laugh during the clash.
Here's to the pin, the brave and bold,
With stories waiting to be told!

Echoes of Bravery.

They say the heart of courage glows,
A badge of valiance, I suppose.
My trusty pin, it hangs a bit,
But still on me it likes to sit!

In battles fought with spoon and fork,
I wear it proudly as I talk.
It winks at foes, it laughs at fate,
Then hides away, it's quite the trait!

Each tale it carries, oh so grand,
Of half-baked plans and grains of sand.
Though I may fumble, trip, or fall,
It's there to catch me through it all!

With laughter echoing in the air,
This token laughs without a care.
For boldness thrives in silly ways,
With hearts adorned in fun-filled praise!

Glistening Shield of Courage

A shiny token, small yet spry,
It gleams and twinkles—oh my, my!
When fears arise, I can't avoid,
This silly glimmer feels employed!

It fights off doubt with pure delight,
And dances when it's held up tight.
In coffee spills or pudding fights,
It stands with me on crazy nights!

Though it may seem a mundane thing,
It's got a power, oh the zing!
The laughter bubble it awakes,
In every scoop of frosted cakes!

So cheers for pins and charms of cheer,
That spark the joy and turn the fear!
They're tiny shields in the fun parade,
Adorning brav'ry, unafraid!

Emblems of the Fearless Heart

Oh, wear the symbol of bravado bright,
Though it sometimes itches—what a sight!
This quirky charm on my old coat,
Is proof of courage, but it won't float!

In silly escapades, it finds its way,
To save my day, in its own sway.
I swing it 'round in whimsical glee,
As I brave the depths of my own tea!

Every badge has its tale to share,
Of funny moments and occasional scare.
So let's raise a glass for silly things,
For laughter is what true brav'ry brings!

So if you spot a sparkly gleam,
Just think of all the fun we dream.
With hearts adorned, let's play our part,
Emblems cherished—fearless heart!

www.ingramcontent.com/pod-product-compliance
Lightning Source LLC
Chambersburg PA
CBHW050031130526
44590CB00042B/2511